Praying Through the Pandemic:

Ignite Your Faith
and
Conquer Your Fears

by

Garnet Nowell

Printed in the United States of America
First Printing: 2021

Published by Inspiration Flows
Broken Arrow, OK 74012
www.inspirationflows.com

Cover design: Copyright © 2021 CANVA

Table of Contents

Dedication

This book is dedicated to the thousands who have lost the battle with Covid-19 and to their families, healthcare workers, first responders, and others who were deeply impacted by this pandemic. The Holy Spirit inspired me to write this book with the collaboration of some of my dearest friends and sisters in the Lord. These women are prayer warriors who know how to fight in the Spirit, decree the Word and expect miracles. Please join us as we pray through this pandemic.

Acknowledgements

Many thanks to my friends and family members who contributed to this book:

Shanedra Nowell

Eve Washington

Delphine Riley

Rosa Campbell

Shantel Nelson

Yvette Lanier

Kristen Cook

Karis Iron

Victoria Whitaker

Introduction

Who would have believed we would be in a global pandemic with deaths in the hundreds of thousands, thousands critically ill, and hospitals overflowing? We need the prayers of the saints more than ever. Jesus told us to draw near to Him in order for Him to abide in us, as we abide in Him (John 15:4). This global pandemic has caused many in the body of Christ to become oppressed and afraid. God never meant for us to be afraid. In fact, according to some scholars, the words *fear not* are found in the Bible 365 times. That is one fear not to cover us for the entire year.

To send pandemic fear packing, God gave us His Word and taught us how to defeat that beast through prayer. These pandemic prayers will provoke faith in you, not fear.

The Oxford Dictionary defines a pandemic as an outbreak of an infectious disease prevalent over a whole country or world. Pervasive, widespread, rampant, global, and universal are other adjectives associated with a pandemic. One of the most significant challenges in facing a pandemic is dealing with the significant toll it makes on our balance of life. Suddenly, physical well-being is imminently threatened; concern for ourselves and our loved ones

escalates; impact on our financial well-being may happen, and our spiritual health may be tested as we deal with isolation and heavy burdens of prayer needs. For these reasons, it is crucial for us to remember that first and foremost, we are called to believe, pray and proclaim a spiritual harvest in the midst of a pandemic. Let's pray.

Healthcare Workers
by Garnet Nowell

Father, we look to you; we know our help comes from you. Lead, guard, and protect our healthcare workers. Let them rely on you as well as on the science you created and govern. For those who do not have a relationship with you, lead your people across their path that they may come to know you as Lord and Savior. Give them the wisdom to know what to do in every situation. I pray they remain healthy and that no sickness shall come near them, and any virus which tries to attach itself to their bodies must instantly die. Father, teach them how to lay hands on the sick and pray

with the authority you have given them. Your Word says that we are already healed, so Father, thank you that we rely on and trust your word. Covid-19 is just a name, and with anything named, it must submit to your authority. At the name of Jesus, Covid-19 must bow. Lord, you sent your Word, and your Word does not return void but accomplishes whatever it was sent to do. Therefore, we boldly proclaim that healthcare workers are protected, and their patients are healed in Jesus' name. We command every fowl, filthy demonic spirit that tries to attack and discourage our healthcare workers to submit to the Word's authority and flee; we release angels to go

and procure all that these workers need, including protective gear and manpower to defeat this enemy. Thank you for the manifestation of miraculous healings, signs, and wonders. In Jesus' name, Amen.

First Responders
by Garnet Nowell

Father, during the pandemic, we pray for police officers and first responders all around the world. Lord, we thank you that you lean down and listen to our prayers. You have called first responders to protect and serve, and you have gifted them with everything they need to do their jobs. Thank you for all the training they have received in order to help others. Father, we thank you for protecting them from the virus and from any schemes the enemy may try to use against them. Let them know that you have not given them a spirit of fear, but you have given them power, love, and soundness so

mind during this difficult time. We thank you that the angels of God surround them and protect them. Father, in these perilous times when we are asked by government officials to practice social distancing to prevent the spread of this Covid-19, give us the wisdom to know how to pray for first responders in their time of need. For those who daily put their lives on the line for us, please give them the wisdom to provide adequate support where needed. Amen

Teachers and School Officials
by Garnet Nowell

Father, this has been a difficult time for teachers and school administrators. They have been asked to rethink how to teach and how to govern. Thank you that they have the mind of Christ and know what to do in all situations. Father protect them from Covid-19 and let them know they are safe in your care. Give them wisdom as they prepare to return to class or to teach virtually. Jesus, the greatest of all teachers, reminds us that He abides in them as they abide in Him. Teach them how to teach and govern with love, patience, and authority. Father, thank you for protecting the children they have in

their care. Thank you that they have the grace to help all of their students, especially those who are struggling. Give them courage, knowledge, and understanding so they will not be overwhelmed, but Father, overwhelm them with your love, mercy, and grace as they navigate through this season. In Jesus' name, Amen.

Teachers and Students
by Shanedra Nowell

Heavenly Father,

We thank you for all your wonderful gifts, including the grace and protection you've granted us during this pandemic. You've been our Comforter, Friend, Healer, and Guide, and we are forever grateful. We come before you today to lift up our teachers, students, and all those involved in the education of our youth. As a teacher, I know the burdens we often carry as we care for our students—praying they are clothed, fed, protected, and loved at home. The pandemic has presented families with so many challenges with the loss of jobs, homes, and

even loved ones. But we also know and have faith that our God is bigger than these challenges. Thank you, Lord, for being our Provider and we pray that you will continue to bless, keep, heal, and provide for students and their families.

We also pray for the health and protection of teachers. Many educators across the country have lost their lives to coronavirus, and families, schools, and communities feel these losses greatly. As teachers return to the classroom or work tirelessly to prepare lessons for distance learning, we pray that you will give them strength and wisdom to make the right decisions for their students. We pray for health, healing, and divine

protection as they prepare to teach the next generation.

In Jesus' name we pray, Amen!

Those in Authority
by Garnet Nowell

1 Timothy 2:1-4 admonishes us, "First of all, then, I urge that petitions (specific requests), prayers, intercessions (prayers for others) and thanksgivings be offered on behalf of all people, for [kings and all who are in [positions of] high authority, so that we may live a peaceful and quiet life in all godliness and dignity. This [kind of praying] is good and acceptable and pleasing in the sight of God our Savior, who wishes all people to be saved and to come to the knowledge and recognition of the [divine] truth.

As believers, we ask that You give us leaders who are wise and who love and honor You. We pray that they seek answers to the questions being asked concerning the pandemic, the vaccine, and the recovery efforts. We believe that You gave us what we asked for, and therefore we will live in a quiet and peaceful land. As a priority, we consecrate ourselves to come into Your presence. We are privileged to have the ability to come before You with our petitions without fear, as well as the privilege to vote for our leaders. We come offering thanks for our government officials and gratitude for their service. We come without prejudice toward anyone, whether Democrat,

Republican or other political affiliations seeking Your continued blessings on each of them. They need your guidance in this time of crisis to know what to do and when to do it. Father give them Godly wisdom. Teach them to look to You for answers. Father, I pray they are protected from all enemies, whether foreign or domestic. We decree that the angels surround them, and your Holy Spirit guides them into all truth. We command the enemy to withdraw from any plans and schemes against them. We speak victory over this pandemic in the name of Jesus. Amen.

Healing Promise
by Shantel Nelson

We are so thankful for your promises, your ways, and your thoughts. You said within your Word, your thoughts are not our thoughts, neither are your ways our ways. For that, Lord, we are grateful.

We live in some horrific times and fear has been at an all-time high as we walk each day during this pandemic, which has invaded our land. Lord, we know this pandemic was not a surprise to you.

You said in Your Holy Word, if any of you lack wisdom, let him ask of God, that giveth to all men liberally, and upbraided not, and

it shall be given him. That is why we seek your wisdom on how to maneuver each day during this pandemic.

You said to not fear, for you are with us, Lord, please show us how and not to be dismayed. Lord, please teach us, for you are our God. You said you would strengthen us and help us, Lord, thank you. You said you would uphold us with your righteous right hand, and Lord, we trust you.

Father, help us to lean on you even more during these times, not only for our peace and strength but also for all those we encounter daily. As we rise each morning, Lord, we are asking you to search us, O God,

and know our hearts. Try us, O God and know our anxious thoughts and see if there be any way of pain in us and lead us in an everlasting way. We choose to trust you today and every day as we lay the cares of this pandemic into your hands. Be still, my soul! Be still and know that He is God! In Jesus' precious name, Amen!!

Healing Commands
by Delphine Riley

Father, I thank you that Isaiah 53:5 tells us that He was wounded for our transgressions, He was bruised for our iniquities; the chastisement for our peace was upon Him, and by His stripes we are healed. Therefore, I decree that no weapon formed against me shall prosper. No sickness, disease, or plague shall come nigh my dwelling because I am the healed of the Lord. I curse every negative symptom that would try to show up in my body, and I command my body to lineup with the Word and function the way it was created to function. I use my authority as a believer to

lay hands on my body and call it whole, nothing missing, and nothing broken in Jesus' Name. Thank you, Lord, that we have what we say, and I say I am healed in Jesus' name. Amen.

Complete Healing from Covid by Garnet Nowell

Father, we come to you asking that you heal those affected by Covid-19. We know you are Jehovah Rapha, the God who heals. Our healing was provided for through the shed blood of our Lord and Savior, Jesus Christ. We were healed by His stripes. We pray for your perfect peace in this situation. Covid-19 is not above the name of Jesus and at the name of Jesus, everything must bow, and we now see Covid-19 bowing and leaving the body. Your Word declares our bodies are fearfully and wonderfully made. We are manifesting the image and presence of God.

Our body is free from fear, sickness, or disease. In Jesus' name. Amen.

Thank You, Father for Healing
by Rosa Campbell

Father, we come to you in the name of
Jesus. We enter into your throne with
thanksgiving in our hearts for all that you
have done through Jesus. Father, you said
in your Word, where there are 2 or 3
gathered together in your name, there you
are, and right now we thank you, Father,
that you are in the midst of us. We thank
you that there is no distance in prayer.
Father, we thank you for the blessings you
have given us and for the many more that
await us. Father, we come into your throne
room; we thank you for health and healing.
Father, right now, with the authority that we

have in Jesus' name, we speak to my
brother's body, his lungs to line up with the
Word of God. Inflammation in the lungs,
gone in the name of Jesus. Lungs, we
command you to expand right now in the
name of Jesus. Cough, we command you to
stop in the name of Jesus. Body, we call you
strong in Jesus' name. Satan, you take your
hands off of my brother Gonzalo's body. You
have no place nor authority over him. We
call Gonzalo's body completely healed and
whole in Jesus' name. Father, we thank you
that we can come boldly and ask these
things and know without a shadow of a
doubt that you hear us, and we have the
petitions we bring. Father, we thank you for

your Word that it is forever established in heaven. You never change, Glory to God! That same power that rose Jesus from the dead is right now working in Gonzalo's body, Glory to God! I thank you, Father, for Your anointing on Gonzalo's body that it is causing a healing and a cure. Father, we choose to believe your report and not dwell on the report of the doctors. Father, we thank you for all the doctors and nurses, technicians involved in my brother's care. We ask Holy Spirit to guide them every step of the way and on what treatments and medications they should give to my brother. Holy Spirit guide Gonzalo as he does his breathing treatments. Anxiety we speak to

you right now, leave in Jesus' name. Father, I thank you that you are ever-present, Glory to God! Father, we ask for peace in Gonzalo's heart and mind that he knows that you are always with him, right next to him and that he knows that you never leave him nor forsake him. Father, I thank you that he will have a good night's rest and wake up in the morning alert and with supernatural strength. Thank you, Father. We will forever give you praise; we will always glorify the name above all names Jesus. In Jesus' name, we pray Amen.

*Dedicated to her brother, Gonzalo

Prayer Decrees
by Eve Washington

Father, in the name of Jesus we come to you with praise and thanksgiving. I give you all the Glory, Honor, Power, and Adoration unto you the Most-High God because Your mercy endures forever!!!!

You said that you would never leave me nor forsake me, and I stand believing, receiving, and decreeing your Word over me now in the Name of Jesus!

God, I trust you and come boldly before the throne of grace declaring your Word that you are the Lord God, my shepherd, and I do not want. I decree, there is no lack in any

area of my life because you are Jehovah
JIREH, my Provider. I decree that I shall
not be ashamed in the evil time, and in the
days of famine, I shall be satisfied. Thank
you, God, that You sent your Word and
healed me and delivered me from every
form of destruction. Hallelujah! I decree by
your stripes I am healed, and I plead the
Blood of Jesus over every area of my life and
everything that's divinely attached to my life
in the Name of Jesus. I decree no sickness,
disease, or plaque shall come nigh my
dwelling. There shall no evil befall me,
neither shall any plague come nigh my
dwelling. Thank you, God, for giving Your
angels charge over me to keep me in all thy

ways. I have been redeemed from the curse of the law, sickness, and disease, and I am covered in the Blood of Jesus.

I decree that I have the mind of Christ, the Holy Spirit leads me on every decision I make, and I will not lean unto my own understanding, and I choose to trust and believe your Word Only! I decree I am established in righteousness, and oppression is far from me, and NO weapons form against me shall prosper in the Name of Jesus! I decree and thank you, God, for surrounding me with your supernatural Favor, Love, Peace, Joy, and Wisdom. I decree that I walk in health, total wholeness, and healing and prosper even as my soul

prospers because of your Word I am decreeing over my life in the Name of Jesus! I decree that I am your righteous one and shall prosper and flourish like a palm tree, and there is no lack in my life, my house, and my finances in the Name of Jesus! Now I command the angels of the Lord to harken unto the voice of the Lord which is His Word that I have decreed and declared out of my mouth, TO GO AND BRING ALL OF THESE DECREES TO PAST IN THE NAME OF JESUS. AMEN.

Job Security
by Garnet Nowell

Father, I thank you for being my Jehovah Jireh, my Provider. Your Word says that you will supply every need, that you always have a ram waiting in the bush, and that you know our end from our beginning. Father, we trust you with our job, our life, and all that you have given us. I thank you that we walk in divine favor on our jobs or in the job market. Thank you for opening doors of opportunity at every turn and closing those doors which are not meant for us. Give us wisdom as we work or as we proceed in our job search. We are putting our trust in You as you order our steps. We speak safety in

the workplace, and we speak health and wholeness to our body and mind as we navigate through this pandemic. In Jesus' name, Amen.

Godly Wisdom
by Garnet Nowell

Father, I am not concerned or worried because I allow Your Word to penetrate my heart and fill me with faith instead of fear. I lay every burden at Your feet because I know you care for me. You said if I lacked wisdom, I should ask for it, and you will give it generously to all without reproach.

Father, I thank you that I am wise and that I have knowledge and understanding in the affairs of my life. I trust in the Lord with all my heart and do not lean on my own understanding. I follow the paths of righteousness as you have taught me. Father teach my mouth to speak words of kindness

and my heart to rule with love. Thank you, Father, for giving me the wisdom that comes from above that is pure, peace-loving, courteous (considerate, gentle), willing to yield to reason, full of compassion and good fruits, wholehearted and straightforward, impartial, and free from doubts, wavering, and insincerity. Thank you for giving me the wisdom and understanding needed to remain firm in my faith during this pandemic. In Jesus' name, Amen.

Against Worry and Fear
by Kristen Cook

Father, thank you that we do not have to live with worry and fear. We are surrounded by your sweet peace and comfort in every area of our lives. You are—ALWAYS—there to listen, and there is nothing we cannot bring to you in prayer. In Jesus' name, amen.

Peace and Protection
by Karis Iron

Dear Heavenly Father,

Thank you for your peace and protection. Thank you that we do not have a spirit of fear but love, power, and a sound mind.

In Jesus Name, Amen.

Situational Awareness
by Garnet Nowell

Father, I seek your face. Please show me what is hidden and reveal any secret agendas that the enemy has planned. Stop any attacks from my enemies, whether human or supernatural. Father, I thank you that you teach my hands to war, not with weapons of flesh, but with spiritual weapons created to tear down anything that comes up against me.

I thank you that I possess supernatural insight into the spiritual world, and I see with the eyes of my spirit and hear with my spiritual ears. No weapon formed against me shall prosper, and anything that tries to

come against me your Word says you shall contend with. Thank you, Father God, that I can lay down to sleep at night and sleep soundly knowing You never slumber or sleep but are watching over me. In Jesus' name, Amen.

Overcoming Fear
by Yvette Lanier

Thank You, Heavenly Father, you have not given me a spirit of fear, but one of power, love, and sound mind. In the midst of a pandemic, I chose to cast my anxiety on You as you remind me in this world, we will have trouble and sorrow, but we do not have to be afraid as You have overcome the world. I thank you for being with my family and me as we abide in the shadow of You Heavenly Father. You protect us from all evil, so I do not have to fear. I will choose instead to be strong and of good courage. I will choose to have peace of mind as I trust in your goodness. I know as I walk through the

valley of the shadow of death, I can take comfort in knowing your rod and your staff protects me and my loved ones. Thank you for meeting my needs of peace and comfort each day. Amen in Jesus' Name.

Compassion
by Yvette Lanier

Heavenly Father, In the midst of a pandemic, I cloth myself with compassion for those hurting around me. Many have lost jobs, income and sadly have lost loved ones. Help me show those in my family or neighborhood the love of Christ by reaching out with what I have in my hands and heart, whether it is food, money, clothes, or a Word of encouragement to lift up a weary soul. I will choose to love my neighbor as I love myself and treat others as I would want someone to treat me in this difficult time. Help me share faith and hope with those in need as I build them up with encouragement

and comfort. Thank You for giving me the strength and courage to be a light in the darkness. In Jesus' Name, Amen.

Ephesian Prayers 1:15-23 (AMP)

The Ephesian prayers are powerful statements of faith and trust in our Lord, Jesus Christ. These prayers can be personalized by placing a specific name in the blank spaces. Pray these prayers for yourself or others.

Prayer for spiritual wisdom

For this reason, because I have heard of your faith in the Lord Jesus and your love for all God's people, I do not cease to give thanks for _____, remembering _____ in my prayers; [I always pray] that the God of our Lord Jesus Christ,

the Father of glory, may grant

_____a spirit of wisdom and of
revelation [that gives you a deep and
personal and intimate insight] into the true
knowledge of Him [for we know the Father
through the Son]. And [I pray] that the eyes
of _____heart [the very center
and core of your being] may be enlightened
[flooded with light by the Holy Spirit], so
that you will know and cherish the [a]hope
[the divine guarantee, the confident
expectation] to which He has called you, the
riches of His glorious inheritance in the
[b]saints (God's people), and [so that you
will begin to know] what the immeasurable
and unlimited and surpassing greatness of

His [active, spiritual] power is in

_____ who believes. These are in

accordance with the working of His mighty

strength which He [c]produced in Christ

when He raised Him from the dead and

seated Him at His own right hand in the

heavenly places, far above all rule and

authority and power and dominion [whether

angelic or human], and [far above] every

name that is named [above every title that

can be conferred], not only in this age and

world but also in the one to come. And He

[d]put all things [in every realm] in

subjection under Christ's feet, and

[e]appointed Him as [supreme and

authoritative] head over all things in the

church, which is His body, the fullness of Him who fills and completes all things in all [believers].

Ephesian Prayers 3:14-21 (AMP)

For this reason [grasping the greatness of this plan by which Jews and Gentiles are joined together in Christ] I bow my knees [in reverence] before the Father [of our Lord Jesus Christ], from whom every family in heaven and on earth [a]derives its name [God—the first and ultimate Father]. May He grant _____ out of the riches of His glory, to be strengthened and spiritually energized with power through His Spirit in your inner self, [indwelling your innermost being and personality], so that Christ may dwell in _____ heart(s) through your faith. And may _____, having been [deeply] rooted and [securely]

grounded in love, be fully capable of
comprehending with all the saints (God's
people) the width and length and height and
depth of His love [fully experiencing that
amazing, endless love]; and [that
_____may come] to know
[practically, through personal experience]
the love of Christ which far surpasses [mere]
knowledge [without experience], that you
may be filled up [throughout your being] to
all the fullness of God [so that you may have
the richest experience of God's presence in
your lives, completely filled and flooded
with God Himself]. Now to Him who is able
to [carry out His purpose and] do
superabundantly more than all that we dare

ask or think [infinitely beyond our greatest prayers, hopes, or dreams], according to His power that is at work within us, to Him be the glory in the church and in Christ Jesus throughout all generations forever and ever. Amen.

Overcoming Grief
by Garnet Nowell

Dear Heavenly Father,

Your Word reminds us that you are merciful when we are in distress. You are there when our hearts are broken. You bind broken hearts and mend wounded souls. Father, we pour our hearts to you because you have promised to care for us. You have promised to give us a peace that transcends all understanding, and Father, we need that peace at this time as we grieve. We know we are not alone in this; we know that you have promised never to leave us nor forsake us. Your precious Holy Spirit is even now comforting us so that our hearts may not be

overwhelmed as we put our trust in you.
Thank you for being our hope and our
healer. Amen.

Conspiracy Theories
by Garnet Nowell

Father, we come boldly to your throne of grace, knowing we are always welcome. We do not take this opportunity lightly. Proverbs 6:16-19 declares these six things the Lord hates; indeed, seven are repulsive to Him: A proud look [the attitude that makes one overestimate oneself and discount others], a lying tongue, and hands that shed innocent blood, a heart that creates wicked plans, feet that run swiftly to evil, a false witness who breathes out lies [even half-truths], and one who spreads discord (rumors) among brothers. Father, we know we have authority in the earth to

bind and to loose. We pray that Truth prevails and all the falsehoods and conspiracies being spoken during the pandemic be silenced. Lord, we are your people, and whoever knows You listens to us, but those who do not know You do not listen to us. This is how we recognize the Spirit of Truth from a lying spirit. Lord, Your Word is Truth. We cloth ourselves with the belt of Truth and continually speak against all falsehoods. We know our enemy, and we know he is the Father of lies. We know we have authority over him and all lying demons who try to twist the Truth with just the right amount of Truth to deceive those who do not have wisdom. Thank you

that we are armed with discernment. We know the Spirit of Truth, and He guides us into all the Truth concerning the pandemic. Father, we thank you that you hear our prayers and give us the power to withstand any assault of the enemy during this time. In Jesus' name, Amen.

Spiritual Harvest
by Victoria Whitaker

Heavenly Father, I come to you in the Name of Jesus and thank You for great spiritual harvest during this season being called a pandemic. By faith, I declare that we will sow seeds of prayer for both unbelievers and believers during this time and believe that just as Isaac sowed in a time of famine and reaped in the same year a hundredfold, we know that spiritual harvest will come forth in abundance. I lift up any that may not know Jesus Christ in the forgiveness of sins and pray salvation would come to them. Your Word promises in Acts 2:21, "...whosoever shall call on the name of the

Lord shall be saved" (NKJV). I pray the convicting power of the Holy Spirit would come to them so they may call on You for salvation. Satan, in the name of Jesus, I take authority over your attempts to blind the minds of unbelievers so that they have not seen the light of the gospel of the glory of Jesus Christ, who is the image of God. I decree the light of the living gospel of Jesus Christ shining forth to them. I also ask that they may receive the baptism of Your Holy Spirit with the evidence of speaking in other tongues as You promised in Acts 2:4. Spirit-filled believers receive the greatest blessing of spiritual harvest by receiving eternal life and power to walk with You in this life. We

are instructed to pray for more laborers to be sent out for the plentiful harvest that waits, so I pray that now. You alone Father, know how to touch the heart of each and every unbeliever. You know what laborer is needed for the assignment. We ask that laborers be sent in their path to minister salvation and Holy Spirit baptism. We refuse to be distracted during this pandemic and forget that winning souls is our first responsibility. Thank you for giving us direction on how we can reach others even during times of isolation, quarantining, etc. Whether through phone calls, cards by mail, online posts, and socially distanced greetings behind masks, we can touch lives

during this season called a pandemic. We claim our family members, friends, neighbors, co-workers, and strangers for the kingdom of God! We rejoice now for their salvation. As believers, growing in our knowledge of You Heavenly Father is possible in the middle of a pandemic. We are reminded Jesus expressed His priority before He returned to heaven in Mark 16:15, telling us to go into all the world preaching the gospel to every creature and also in Acts 1:8 when He said we would be witnesses, telling people about Him everywhere. We are grateful You give us wisdom and direction on how to reach out to others with words of life, including encouragement and

hope. Right in the middle of what seems to be a dire time, we can grow in our knowledge of You as we spend time with You reading Your Word and in prayer. We can fellowship with one another through methods other than meeting in person since pandemic restrictions may deny that. We also declare an increase in intimacy with You as we draw near to You and learn of You greater than ever before. I pray we, as Christian believers, will come out of this pandemic spiritually stronger. Thank you for providing us with a strong spirit of prayer and insight on how to pray for ourselves as well as others. We purpose to walk strongly in love and yield to the fruit of

the Spirit as described in Galatians 5:22 –
love, joy, peace, patience, gentleness,
goodness, faith, humility, and self-control.
As Your Spirit leads us, we believe there will
be acts of kindness and compassion we can
demonstrate during this pandemic that
touches others for Your glory. While the
greatest of our signs as believers is our love
for one another, we also declare signs,
wonders, and many miracles that will be
demonstrated in this last day's revival.
Thank you, Heavenly Father, for the gifts of
the Spirit given to the church for a
demonstration of sovereignty and
faithfulness. We realize that a revelation of
Your goodness is paramount to others

receiving You in Your fullness and Your blessings. Jesus clearly told us in John 10:10 the thief is the one who came to steal, to kill, and to destroy, while Jesus came to give life and even more abundant life. James 1:17 promises us, "Every good gift and every perfect gift is from above, and comes down from the Father of lights..." (NIV). We agree in prayer, acknowledging that You are good and that your mercy endures forever. May we be led to release faith-filled words that spark others' faith. There is creative power released when we speak forth words in alignment with Your written Word causing others to respond in faith. May we be sensitive to be used by the Holy Spirit to

help others receive their blessings. In this way, spiritual harvest increases. Godly spiritual harvest also increases when we live an ambassador's lifestyle. Philippians 3:20 mandates that Christian believers are citizens of heaven. As such, we should seek to know the environment of heaven and our covenant rights as followers of Jesus Christ. For example, there is no sickness, disease, poverty, strife, or fear in heaven. Those things are under the curse of the law. I declare in prayer that we are redeemed from the curse of the law and will walk in our covenant benefits. When an ambassador travels to a foreign country, they live in the same lifestyle as the country of their

citizenship. They are recognized as citizens of the country of origin. We purpose in prayer to represent the fullness of Christ in our ambassador lifestyle so others may be drawn to His glory. According to the Word of God, we loose the ministering angels to work on our behalf in bringing about the will of the Father in our lives. Just as ambassadors have assistants to serve them and protect them, we believers have angels at work in our lives. They assist in bringing deliverance, divine appointments, and contacts to us (Hebrews 1:14 and Psalm 91:11-12). We are so thankful to be known as His own and be aware that we may experience a great spiritual harvest during

this pandemic. I release this prayer by faith in the name of Jesus. Amen.

Final Thoughts

You are not alone. God is with you every step of the way. We have been through a lot in the past few months, but we are stronger together.

May God continually bless you and keep you as we constantly push on toward the mark of our higher calling in Christ.

God is so, so good. He desires to a relationship with us; He adores us; and He is always there for us. Trust Him.

Utilize these prayers for your friends, family, co-workers, or anyone you know who needs a touch from our Father. Be Blessed.

Books by Garnet Nowell

Hey, Don't Be That Girl 21-Day Devotional

Hey, Don't Be That Girl Devotional Journal

www.ingramcontent.com/pod-product-compliance
Lightning Source LLC
Chambersburg PA
CBHW071846020426
42331CB00007B/1874